Leadership Frames

Six Frameworks for Analyzing and Enhancing Your Leadership Role

Second Edition

Joseph M. Coyle
Joseph D. Hospital

- 2016 -

To our wives,
Sally and Beverly

Leadership Frames

Second Edition

ISBN 978-0-692-75335-4
Library of Congress Cataloging-in-Publication data is available.

Printed in the United States of America.

Publisher:
BCG Books
Washington, DC

Editor
Sally E. DiPaula

Book and Cover Design
Jeep Watson
410-963-8822

For speaking engagements and training programs,
contact the authors at jcoyle@bcgdc.com

Table of Contents

Introduction

Despite valiant efforts by researchers in recent years, no one has been able to identify universal leadership behaviors or traits. The fact that there is no definitive answer to the question "What is a good leader?" should not surprise us. Amazon.com lists over 10,000 books on management and leadership, and dozens of new titles on the subject appear each month.

Accordingly, in approaching the subject of leadership, we recognize the challenge: There are many paths to better leadership, but there is no one path. To deal with this challenge (or conundrum), most writers go into great detail about one or two elements of leadership. Familiar examples are:

Focus on the strengths of your people.
Get the right people on the bus.
Provide a clear vision for your organization.
Create an entrepreneurial culture that encourages risk taking.
Prepare your people for a constantly changing environment.

Fortunately, the majority of these books contain useful insights, approaches and recommendations that can help all of us to become more effective leaders.

In this book, we take a somewhat different approach: We present six frameworks of analysis by which you can continually monitor and adjust your leadership approaches and behaviors.

An important added benefit of our approach is that leaders appreciate the fact that our frameworks encourage them to be independent and self-directed in carrying out their leadership role.

Before moving into the first framework, we would like to address a question about leadership often overlooked in books on the subject: Why do we need managers and executives? We will begin to answer that question by looking at two kinds of businesses.

1) A Construction Site

Position	Work Done	Measurability
Bricklayers	All well-defined	Very high
Site Manager	Largely ill-defined	Low
Sr. Vice President	Almost exclusively ill-defined	Very low

We would first like to focus on bricklayers, whose work is very well-defined. The bricklayer prepares mortar, lays bricks, and finishes off the surfaces. From experience, it is known how many bricks an experienced person can lay in a shift of eight hours. So a bricklayer has a well-defined job that can be measured and that demands continuous concentration on one or two key tasks. A major benefit to a bricklayer and other such craft people, by the way, is that their days are inherently productive. At the end of the day, they do not have to ask themselves if they added value to the business. It's a given.

But how about the site manager? He does not actually build or erect any part of the buildings; that is, he doesn't do foundation work, install dry wall, or pour concrete. Which leads us back to our question: Why do we need him?

That manager is needed to add value. He has to move beyond paperwork, phone calls and meetings and help drive results at a higher level of the business. For example, he adds value by instituting an improved safety program, finding a less costly trucking company, warning other departments about schedule changes, or identifying ways to increase on-site craft productivity. And when this site manager adds value, he is fulfilling his leadership role.

But there's a problem: Since the manager's work is ill-defined, there is no one way or one formula for completing the added-value work. For example, when coordinating the purchase and delivery of materials to the site, how he does it makes an enormous difference to the business. If he identifies a very reliable trucking company that provides a lower price, he adds value. If the trucking company is unreliable, he may end up undermining the entire construction site effort.

As to the Sr. VP, she may not even visit the construction site. She may be searching for new real estate to develop, pulling together a business proposal, or identifying new sources of building supplies. Her work is largely ill-defined, and so she has to be very careful to ensure that she is adding value to the business at the macro level.

To further illustrate this concept, let's turn to a restaurant.

2) A Restaurant

Position	Work Done	Measurability
Line Cook	All well-defined	Very high
General Manager	Largely ill-defined	Low
Regional VP	Almost exclusively ill-defined	Very low

Again, we can see the pattern. A cook goes home every day knowing that his core work made a genuine difference in the outcome of that restaurant's day. The general manager, on the other hand, does not prepare, cook or serve food. Her primary role is to add value at a higher level: budgeting, marketing, customer relations, employee relations, cost controls—all largely ill-defined activities that can be done in numerous ways and that depend on a wide range of business conditions. The VP is concerned with responsibilities that are even more ill-defined: identifying a new public relations firm, leading a new product development team, analyzing costs.

Therefore, recognizing this fundamental difference between a bricklayer and a site manager or between a cook and a regional vice president, we can describe the primary role a leader must play:

Leaders must complete ill-defined, qualitative work that adds value to the business.

From our experience, doing so is not easy; it is, in fact, quite challenging. Our six frameworks will, we believe, help you meet the challenge.

Frame 1

Moving toward Added-Value Work

Added Value Work

Now that we have focused on the special responsibility a leader has to add value to his or her business, you may be asking yourself, "Isn't this obvious and easy to do?" From our experience, the answer is a resounding "No." And our first formal framework illustrates why:

ROUTINE WORK ➔ "FIRES" ➔ ADDING VALUE

This framework reveals one of the salient leadership challenges of our post-industrial, digital age. Although leaders exist to add value to the business, they face so much routine work and so many fires on a daily basis that finding time to invest in the third column, "adding value" is difficult. Listen to the words of a number of executives with whom we work:

> *"As general manager of a full-service hotel, I need to be adding value all the time. Yet, I have to spend the first four hours of my day, from 8 a.m. to 12 noon, just dealing with emails and routine corporate requests. In fact, some days I work through lunch on this routine work so that I can spend at least a half day leading the hotel in ways that make a difference."*

> *"My most important role is walking this $800 million construction site, observing the work and asking questions about safety, productivity and schedule. Unfortunately, it doesn't happen very often. Just last week, I spent four of the five days in the construction trailer answering emails and finishing the quarterly report to the client. Sometimes I wonder if I am more a clerk than an executive."*

> *"As director of finance for our division, I should be very hands-on with my eight accountants and with the other executive team members, but I get 80 to 120 emails a day. Last Monday, for example, I arrived in my office to see 150 emails on my desktop. Some of these require a lot of thought; others require conversations with my accountants. It can take me two days to catch up properly. It's very frustrating."*

These observations are not unusual; in fact, they are typical. The majority of managers and executives tell us that it is very difficult to find time to add value to their business even though they believe that their responsibility is to do just that.

Your Turn

To further this analysis, we would like you to fill out the first two columns of the chart. That is, list what you believe are routine tasks in your job and what are unplanned "fires" that arise during any day or week. Simply write whatever comes to mind. Further along, we provide examples from lists that hundreds of professionals like you have generated in our leadership seminars.

ROUTINE WORK	"FIRES"	ADDING VALUE,

The Importance of Routine Work

Before presenting sample lists, we want to recognize the fact that routine work and "fires" are essential elements of everyone's work life. They must be completed or dealt with. If we didn't fill out trip reports or inform our colleagues via email that a meeting has been rescheduled, attend meetings to show our support for another group or team, etc., the world of work would come to a halt. Rather, our point is this: If your business or organization is to thrive, you must do more than complete routine work and put out "fires."

As a leader, you must find ways to add value while other people are completing the core tasks of your business because those people are completing well-defined work and do not have time for much else. Since they are entering data, nursing patients, collecting monies, installing software, hooking up electricity, auditing balance sheets or waiting on customers, they are relying on you, the leader, to move beyond the here and now and drive the business forward.

Now, we would like to present a list of routine tasks and "fires" gleaned from the input of thousands of managers and executives like you. We hope that the list reflects, at least partially, your own:

ROUTINE WORK	"FIRES"	ADDING VALUE
E-mail	Computer system problems	
Phone calls	Unnecessary interruptions	
Meetings	Customer complaints or problems	
Paperwork	Unscheduled requests for information	
Reports	Mistakes that need addressing	
Conference calls	Employee performance issues	
Filing	Missing resources	

In your list, you may have included routine tasks such as managing the details of your travel, moving from one building to another, getting materials ready for a weekly business meeting, handling visitors to your offices, or waiting for other team members to provide you the data or information you need. Given the wide range of occupations and business conditions under which people work in the digital age, a comprehensive list of routine tasks would be pages long. Fortunately, we find that the leaders we train and coach have a clear idea of what constitutes routine work and "fires." Moreover, we are always amazed at how much consensus exists on the fact that routine work is constantly growing.

As we present these ideas in more detail throughout this book, you may want to rework the lists you have made. But now, we want to turn to a critical step in our leadership process: Identifying what is adding value in your position at this time.

As you read the previous pages, you may have been thinking about the activities that belong in the third column of our framework. To be truly effective in your leadership role, you must, we believe, have a clear idea of what constitutes adding value in your job. The phrase "at this time" is important to this effort because how you add value will vary according to business conditions.

Before inviting you to complete your list, we would like to illustrate adding value in a number of businesses. First, we present general categories that leaders tell us are often critical to driving results in an organization. Then we present more targeted lists.

Added-Value Activities

General

1. Analyzing existing business processes.
2. Thinking creatively to generate new ideas and new services.
3. Proactively recruiting high-quality employees, managers and executives.
4. Engaging in "high-touch" interactions with staff to build morale and gain input.
5. Interacting with existing customers and clients to build the business.
6. Identifying sources of new customers or clients.
7. Identifying ways to increase sales.
8. Reorganizing business units to increase efficiency and effectiveness.
9. Making an important decision involving a number of choices.

Obviously, the items on the above list are very general, but they can serve as a guide for developing your own added-value list that is specific and concrete. In that vein, we turn to real-life examples of lists generated by leaders in three separate disciplines. Our goal here is to help you create your own list, which we invite you to do on page 17.

Project Manager

1. Create a draft outline for the new executive development program.
2. Identify three staff members to attend the corporate executive development program and send out invitations.
3. Review the IT software implementation program and make suggestions.
4. Develop a new report framework for communicating with the client.
5. Spend time with the accounting team to help them improve their interactions with other departments.
6. Identify ways to extend business with existing clients.
7. Work with the Safety Coordinator to develop a fresh approach to designing and communicating our safety messages.

National Director of Human Resources

1. Develop a five-year plan to better manage health care costs for the company.
2. Identify three new sources of college interns.
3. Develop a formal succession plan for high-potential managers.
4. Assess and report on the current status of the company's compensation program.
5. Redesign the new employee orientation program to expand its scope and length.
6. Set up a tracking system for the posting and filling of open positions in the company.
7. Develop a plan for integrating into the company the employees who are part of the recent acquisition.
8. Identify ways to streamline the administration of company benefits.

Vice President of Finance

1. Analyze competitors' pricing structures.
2. Evaluate the cost-benefit of the new business opportunity identified.
3. Provide a financial perspective at three regional operations conferences.
4. Identify upcoming changes in market conditions affecting sales.
5. Identify opportunities for improved cost controls in various departments.
6. Begin the annual review of capital expenditure projects.

Your Turn

As you complete your "adding value" list below, keep in mind that you may end up with a mix of what we call micro and macro activities; that is, some will be basic and immediate and others large and long term.

What Constitutes Adding Value in My Position at This Time

1. ______
2. ______
3. ______
4. ______
5. ______
6. ______
7. ______
8. ______

Calibrating

Once you have refined this list to your satisfaction, we recommend that you meet with your boss to calibrate your activities with him or her. In this way, you can be certain that you are spending your time in a way that is valuable to the organization—and valued by your boss. Your boss, in turn, will be reassured that you are attempting to make a real difference in the organization. These added-value lists can also generate useful conversations between the two of you: what obstacles will you face; who needs to be brought into the process; what additional benefits may accrue to the organization; and how long will the activity take to complete.

We use the word "attempting" in the last paragraph for a good reason. As mentioned earlier, most leaders tell us that they struggle mightily to find time to focus on adding value in any given day or week because so much of their time is taken up with routine work and "fires." In fact, on average, managers and executives report spending just 20 percent of their time adding value. However, as we explain later in this book, you should not be discouraged by this percentage, for you can make an enormous impact on your business and on results in just 8 to 10 hours of any week.

Now that you have made your initial list of added-value activities, we would like to present further examples, which may help you extend or refine your list.

Adding Value: Portrait Photographer

For ten years, Alex, the 38-year-old owner of a small photography studio, had been making a good living going to the offices of companies and non-profit organizations and taking high-quality photos of founders, CEOs and other high-level executives.

Although Alex felt good about his success, he told us that he felt he was "burning too much fuel," that is, putting in long days every week. After being encouraged to think of ways to add value to his business, he identified a change he could make. He began offering executives a 40 percent discount on the photo shoot if they would come to his studio for their portraits. Alex had analyzed the effort associated with traveling to the offices of his clients: travel time (40 minutes on average); camera, lighting and background set-up time (1 hour); breakdown and packing of this equipment (45 minutes); and travel time back to the studio (40 minutes). The total: 3 hours plus, not including actual camera time.

The gambit worked. Many clients took Alex up on his offer. He concluded that it wasn't always the money; some execs just wanted to get out of the office for a few hours. Since much of Alex's profit results not from the photo shoot but from clients' purchase of prints in various sizes, his discounting was not damaging to the business. He ended up making the same amount of money but spending significantly less time doing the work. And he reduced his work week by 10 hours.

Alex's simple but powerful change in business process is an example of a one-time, long-term, added-value step. Of course, Alex could be criticized for not analyzing his time and effort years earlier. But in the real world, many of us become stuck in our routine processes simply because they are working for us.

ROUTINE WORK → "FIRES" → ADDING VALUE

Adding Value: Chef

A chef in a high-end restaurant in the Caribbean circulates through the restaurant each evening speaking to diners. He carries promotional cards with him and hands them out to diners. One side of the card presents the recipe for a signature dish, the other side a photo of the restaurant. The chef adds value by interacting with diners and accelerates that value by distributing these recipe cards. Of course, this chef is a busy leader and has, as he says, "tons of work to complete just to keep the kitchen operating." Yet, he is determined to find time to add value to the customer experience—even if it involves only 20 minutes each evening.

Adding Value: Interior Design Senior Manager

Ron Bensen is a senior manager in charge of a major commercial interior design firm. As part of the final turnover process to the client, he and his team would provide several three-inch-thick binders that contained all of the project's drawings and specifications. This hard-copy approach had been in place for years. On his latest project, he decided to send clients only digital records. He was pleasantly surprised that the clients accepted the digital files without a second thought and never mentioned the need for binders with hard copies. The savings in paper, time and effort was substantial.

Add Value on Two Levels

As we exhort you to make every effort to add value, we do not mean to imply that all such efforts should be toward major changes or major improvements in your business. As we alluded to earlier in this chapter, you can view adding value as existing on two levels, illustrated below.

Macro Level

1. A creative way to repackage an existing software product.
2. Removing a significant obstacle to the productivity of every member of a particular department.
3. Identifying a permanent cost-cutting measure that saves millions of dollars a year.
4. Automating a business process (e.g., ATMs and RFIDs) that had previously required thousands of hours of labor annually.

Micro Level

1. Increasing the effectiveness of a weekly staff meeting.
2. Improving the lighting in the offices of your call center.
3. Reducing the frequency requirements of a report.
4. Purchasing more effective headsets for sales staff.
5. Installing better signage for visitors to a large building complex.

Added Value Initiatives: Often a Sunburst

Appreciating the fact that adding value runs the gamut from the seemingly insignificant to the truly grand is important because we find that a leader's mind generates valuable ideas, solutions and insights in a random fashion. One minute we find ourselves thinking about our filing system and a few minutes later about how to completely redesign our software development organization. Good ideas that add value to your business will pop up randomly. In fact, if you demand of yourself that you generate only big ideas, you may end up frustrating the creative process.

For example, we observed a CEO visiting one of her departments and asking about the worn carpet on the floor of the offices. She was there to discuss the redesign of an advertising campaign, a major decision for the company. Nevertheless, this small detail attracted her attention, and she did not want to let it go. Even before going into the meeting, she encouraged the office manager to improve the work environment by installing new carpet that would be cleaner and brighter. This CEO's experience is not unusual given that valuable ideas often come as a sunburst, unexpected but welcomed.

Your Turn

Observing Added-Value Improvements

Can you identify two or three macro-level added-value improvements and three micro-level improvements that have occurred in your business or organization over the past six months to a year? They can be ones generated by you or by co-workers.

Macro Level

1. ______________________________

2. ______________________________

3. ______________________________

Micro Level

1. ______________________________

2. ______________________________

3. ______________________________

Other Ways to View Adding Value

The breakdown we have just presented represents just one way of approaching an analysis of added-value work. There are, of course, a myriad of ways to categorize these tasks, interactions and innovations. To stimulate your thinking in this area, we present another categorization, which we feel is straightforward and functional: Recurring vs. One-Shot.

Recurring

Intense Interaction

One of the responsibilities of Trisha Bonaventura as a regional manager for one of America's major casual dining restaurant chains is to visit each of her ten restaurants every two weeks. For years, she had been making these rounds on her own. As a result of a suggestion made in one of our leadership training programs, she decided to invite each general manager (managing just one restaurant) to join her on her bi-weekly tour of the district. For an entire day, the two drive from restaurant to restaurant, giving the general manager a chance to observe Trisha's interactions with the managers of the other nine restaurants in her district. In addition, during these rides, Trisha and the general manager have a chance to chat about food cost control, recruiting of kitchen staff, local store marketing and other important elements of the business. Following this approach, Trisha is able to spend one quality day with each of her general managers over a six-month period.

This is clearly an added-value activity on the part of Trisha. In fact, she considers this day so valuable that she gives herself 100 percent on her productivity score sheet (addressed in the upcoming chapter). Yet, this represents an ongoing commitment of time and effort on her part. Accordingly, we label this added-value activity as "recurring" because the leader has to carry out the activity repeatedly.

Logistics

John Stratton works as a field supervisor for an environmental recycling company. His teams run a series of household waste collection and recycling programs in mid-sized U.S. cities. On Saturdays, residents bring in old cans of paint, various kinds of solvents, lawn pesticides, unused gasoline, car batteries, etc., which they would otherwise discard in the regular trash. Saturday collections are popular, with hundreds of people driving up to each recycling staging area to unload their materials.

As residents drive into the collection area, John's crews unload the items from the cars and trucks and move them to the bins and drums into which everything is packed for shipment to a central processing center.

> After running these collections for more than a year, John realized that the collection process could be improved. His crew members were carrying containers, batteries, etc., 90 feet or more from the vehicles to the recycling staging area. He decided to purchase sturdy rolling carts so that his team could simply place the materials on the carts and roll them to the staging area. With this one step came a number of benefits: less spilling of liquids, fewer broken bottles, fewer back injuries to the crew (who were often carrying heavy items) and faster service.
>
> Moreover, John realized that despite everyone's best efforts, there were occasional spills and breakage, so he purchased large plastic liners to cover the entire work area. As a result, crew clean-up time decreased by 30 minutes and the clients (local governments) were pleased by the fact that the public areas used for the program were left in very good condition.

Although John's team has to lay down the liners and maneuver the carts each week, the benefits are substantial: less work, fewer injuries, and a cleaner, faster service.

One Shot
A Library Room

> The vice president of program development for a major U.S. credit card company heard from his people again and again that the cubicle culture in which they worked made it difficult for them at times to sustain focused, concentrated work that was essential to their productivity. As a result, he created a "library room" within his regional office, where staff could work without interruption or noise. This special room, with desktop computers, printers and comfortable chairs, was a quiet, cell-free, interruption-free zone and was fully enclosed. This oasis was so popular that the staff requested that a second one be created within the office complex.

This is clearly an example of a one-shot added-value action; that is, once constructed, the rooms operated without further input or effort on the part of the vice president.

Golf Course Business Extension

Investors developed a golf course in a relatively rural area about a 45-minute drive from a major U.S. city. The course was challenging, well maintained and rated highly by golfers. Nevertheless, the operation was not meeting the investors' ROI (return on investment). Golf course management intensified their marketing, advertising and promotions, but the increase in sales was not sufficient. In one year, the course lost almost $400,000. Then along came a new golf manager, who was one of those leaders who set aside time for analysis and thinking. Standing to the side of the club house on the top of a hill overlooking the course, he realized that the view was itself of great value. He convinced the owners to build a banquet pavilion, which included a bank of French doors and a patio that showcased the stunning vista. Not only did the facility garner a significant amount of wedding business but also corporate outings, family reunions, birthday parties, bar/bat mitzvahs, anniversary celebrations and the like. Word spread so fast that within two years, the operation showed a profit of $300,000. The new Director of Golf's added-value thinking led to a one-time investment that saved the enterprise.

A Helpful Tool

A hotel department manager was genuinely interested in finding ways to reduce the strains and stresses associated with her housekeepers' job. She embraced the responsibility of analyzing their work and identifying ways to do so. One day, she was inspecting a room as a housekeeper was finishing up the cleaning of the bathtub and shower area. Noticing that the woman was in an awkward position while cleaning the tile and the far side edge of the bathtub, she wondered if there wasn't a better way to do this demanding task. She contacted one of her suppliers and found that there was a mop affixed to a telescopic pole which allowed the user to remain standing at a distance while cleaning the entire tub and shower area. Once the housekeepers were able to use this tool, they found that the strain on their bodies was significantly less and the number of slip and fall accidents was reduced. In this instance, both the housekeeping staff and the hotel benefited from adding value to an existing work process.

Wine Bar Coaster

> At one of the annual conferences where we present on leadership, a beverage manager submitted the following to an "Idea Exchange" exhibit: an information-rich drink coaster developed for wine glasses. On the coaster (which is square rather than round) is printed information on the wine: the name (e.g., pinot grigio), the vintage, the place of origin, a description of its taste (e.g., woody, smooth with a hint of strawberries and currants) and the cost of taking a bottle home. On the opposite side is the website of the bar. So instead of a standard coaster that would be thrown away, the customer gets a souvenir that can be taken home and shared with friends and family. Of course, the coaster also promotes the bar business.

This simple, inexpensive "product" is another example of adding value to a well-established process.

A Big-Shot One Shot

> Periodically, we are fortunate to see a one-shot added-value action that has an enormous impact on society in general. In 2007 the U.S. Postal Service decided to create a "forever" first-class stamp. For decades, they had produced new stamps each time they raised rates—and sometimes had to produce other stamps (2-cent ones, for example) to enable customers to match the increase. The cost savings associated with this new generic stamp will be enormous over time. And it's a step that the Postal Service will not have to take ever again.

Clearly, then, some added-value activities or actions require repetition while others require just a single effort yet create long-term, even permanent, change. However, though all of us would like to take one step and change our work circumstances forever, we should not be discouraged by the need for recurring added-value improvements that require our continual attention. After all, it is just one more reason why we are important to our company or organization.

Frame 2

Workplace Productivity

Adding Value and Productivity

Now that we have laid out our view that the primary responsibility of a leader is to add value to his or her business as often as possible, we would like to present a scoring framework that will help you monitor and evaluate your adding-value efforts on a regular basis.

To begin this discussion, we would like to present the typical productivity scores of thousands of leaders who have participated in our leadership programs.

Weekly Productivity Scores

Monday	Tuesday	Wednesday	Thursday	Friday
60	80	100	100	50

By way of these scores, thousands of managers and executives have told us that they are able to add value and drive results in their business or organization three days a week. They have also told us that Mondays and Fridays are full of routine work, "fires," and, unfortunately, frustration at "not getting enough good work done."

These scores were generated in response to a question asked in our training program: How productive do you feel you were each day last week? The criterion is simple: The more value you added, the higher your daily score. The scoring that lies behind this framework is, of course, impressionistic. But we encourage leaders to follow this approach:

Scores of 80 to 100	indicate that you added value to your business.
Scores of 60 to 79	indicate that you successfully completed your routine work and handled "fires," but had no time to invest in adding value.
Scores below 60	indicate that you could neither do a good job of handling routine work and "fires" nor find time to add value.

To illustrate how leaders score themselves, we present a few vignettes.

Regional Manager in Information Technology

"My boss had me attend a 4-hour meeting with her on Tuesday, and it was a complete waste of time. The vendor who was presenting didn't know much about our company or our needs, and we don't really need the software they sell anyway. By the time my boss and I had lunch and got back to the office, it was after 2 p.m. and all I could do was answer some phone calls and get myself refocused. My score for the day was a 30, which may actually be generous."

General Manager, Full-Service Restaurant

"Last Wednesday, two of my servers were sick with the flu and could not come to work. I ended up spending the whole evening working as a server. Since I'm not used to doing that work, it was tough and tired me out. My score for Wednesday was a 40 because I played almost no leadership role at all for the restaurant team or for our customers."

Financial Consulting Vice-President

"About 11 a.m. last Friday, I was tackling the 60 emails that had piled up during the week and had to answer 7 phone messages that were on my system when one of my best performing consultants interrupted me. She wanted to talk about her job. Although I was tempted to put her off, I asked her to sit down. As it turned out, she was seriously considering quitting. Her heavy travel schedule was taking her away from her husband and 4-year-old daughter, and she was not happy about it. We talked for 45 minutes and ended with my commitment to help her, explaining that we definitely did not want to lose an employee of her caliber. A week later, her manager and I identified a special project that she could work on 50 percent of her time and that involved no travel. She was very pleased and is now in great spirits. My score for the day I set aside my routine work and listened to her needs: 100."

IT Help Desk Senior Manager

> *"While visiting our Help Desk team one afternoon, I noticed that one of the team was rubbing lotion all over her neck, arms and hands. She told me that her skin was always dry and itchy at work, and it distracted her quite a bit. So, the next day I contacted an HVAC consulting firm, who tested the air quality in the Help Desk area and found that the humidity levels were low, around 25 percent. The ideal level is about 50 percent. We bought two humidifiers, which did the trick. A couple of weeks later in a staff meeting, over half the team reported that they had fewer headaches, less dry skin and felt more alert than ever before. My score for the day we set up those humidifiers: 100."*

Your Turn

Before further discussing daily productivity in detail, we invite you to score yourself on your previous work week. (The score sheet includes Saturday and Sunday for those of you who do not work the standard week.)

Your Weekly Productivity Scores

Monday	Tuesday	Wednesday	Thursday	Friday	Saturday	Sunday

The "Soup" Problem

If you had difficulty remembering what you did on certain days, you are not alone. Most leaders can clearly recall only one or two days. For example, if on a Wednesday we ask a group of managers or executives the question, "How productive were you last week?" the majority respond that they cannot even remember the details of the previous Wednesday or Thursday. Many remember incidents or parts of one or two days. The week is often a blur:

> *"I know that I attended a budget meeting last week, but I'm not sure what day it was."*
>
> *"Last Monday, Tuesday and Wednesday are a blank, but I think I attended some useful meetings on Thursday."*
>
> *"I remember that we submitted the quarterly report to the executive committee on Wednesday, but I can't remember what I did that afternoon or the next day."*
>
> *"Without my digital calendar, I really can't do this scoring."*

We refer to this inability to recall previous work experience as the "soup" syndrome because the work week runs together like a pureed soup, in which all the ingredients and colors blend into an undefined mass.

Here's why this is not a good situation: We cannot benefit from a work week that has the feel of soup. Since we can't be sure on which days we were effective, we do not learn from our successes. Nor do we learn from mistakes or opportunities missed. The information is simply not available.

Here's the good news: If you, the leader, can find just one minute at the end of a day to keep a productivity score, the situation improves. In fact, we find that when a manager or executive is asked questions about appointments and meetings listed in the calendar, he or she will not only begin recalling what transpired but will provide interesting insights into the value—or lack of value—of particular events or interactions. So taking one or two minutes to process the day's experience can be time well spent. You'll not only know when you were productive—or not—you'll also know what factors and conditions affect your productivity.

Lastly, just by remembering what you did, your sense of job satisfaction will increase because you will appreciate the ways you added value to your team and organization.

Learning from Your Scores

Having scored the past week of work, you can now address two fundamental questions that will enable you to benefit from your analysis:

What enabled you to be productive on certain days?

1. What were the external factors?
2. What were the internal factors?

What prevented you from being productive on certain days?

1. What were the external factors?
2. What were the internal factors?

Your Turn

Below is a list of conditions, factors and behaviors that leaders report help contribute to their high productivity days. We invite you to check those that fit your circumstances—and add those that we do not list:

- [ ] There was uninterrupted time, which allowed me to concentrate on important work.
- [ ] I was assertive with others and protected my time.
- [ ] My energy level was high.
- [ ] My mood was very positive.
- [ ] My staff provided me just the right materials, information, etc., I needed.
- [ ] There was a deadline that had to be met.
- [ ] I was very interested in the work I was doing.
- [ ] The other team members were well prepared and on target.
- [ ] Because so much good preliminary work was done, I was able to add value.

- [ ] It was simply one of those days when I was very focused and determined.
- [ ]
- [ ]
- [ ]
- [ ]

Some of what makes us productive is external (e.g., no interruptions, good preliminary work) and some internal (e.g., good mood, high energy level). It is important to know which of these is contributing to your productivity and to what degree—given that strategies for each one are often quite different. For example, you may need to establish an exercise routine so that you have more energy (internal) or you may need to train a staff member to handle all of your travel logistics (external) so you can focus on other matters.

Below is a list of conditions, factors and behaviors that leaders tell us often prevent them from having high productivity days. Again, we invite you to check those that fit your circumstances—and add those not listed:

- [ ] I was interrupted regularly during the day.
- [ ] I had so many e-mails and phone calls to deal with that my day never really got going.
- [ ] I had to attend a meeting that was not useful and that took me "off my game."
- [ ] I allowed other people to distract me from my work.
- [ ] I had too many other things on my mind.
- [ ] My energy level was low.
- [ ] My mood was low.
- [ ] My staff did not provide me the materials and information I needed.
- [ ] There was a computer system slowdown or failure.
- [ ] The work or task simply didn't interest me.
- [ ] Not enough meeting pre-work had been done.
- [ ] One or two "fires" came up and my day was pretty much wrecked.

- [ ] My boss had me work on other matters, so I never got back to my own goals for the day.
- [ ] The regional team asked for more information and data, and assembling it took up much of my day.
- [ ]
- [ ]
- [ ]
- [ ]

Your Turn

Now that you have identified those conditions, etc., that can reduce your productivity, we invite you to write down steps you can take to improve your situation.

E.g., I will reduce the number of interruptions, especially in the morning, by setting a couple of hours of "closed door" time.

I am going to identify two or three meetings that I can stop attending each week to give me more time to spend with my programmers.

1.

2.

3.

4.

5.

6.

Scoring Productivity = Processing Your Experience

When you take a minute or two at the end of each day to evaluate your productivity, what you are doing, in a grander sense, is processing your experience. That is, you are creating a sharp awareness of how you are interacting with the world around you. Those adults who keep a daily journal or those who discuss their day in some detail with family or friends over a relaxed dinner are taking the same step. And one advantage to our scoring approach is that it takes little time and effort.

Productivity Scoring in Outlook

> Carlos Ramirez, a program analyst working in Puerto Rico, sets a daily 6:00 p.m. reminder in his Outlook. Carlos reports, "I take only a minute to go over my day, decide if I've added value, and give myself a score. What I like about this scoring is that it often reminds me how productive I've been and makes me feel good about the contribution I'm making to the company. And even when my score is not high, say 60, I realize that I finished a lot of routine work and feel good about that, too."
>
> And since Carlos has a digital file of his scores, he can share them easily with his boss every couple of weeks. His boss, in turn, can discuss the scores and identify ways to help remove obstacles to Carlos' productivity.

The goal of this effort is to identify those factors, internal and external, that enhance or hinder your productivity. The benefit of this scoring cannot be overstated. This reflection (or processing) allows you to know when and how you are adding value to the business. And there's a secondary benefit: Even if you're having a bad day, becoming aware of the reasons can give you a sense of being in control—which may reduce your level of frustration.

The Average Work Week

We would like to return to our average weekly score sheets and provide you some detail about what creates this pattern of scores for thousands of leaders like you:

Monday	Tuesday	Wednesday	Thursday	Friday
60	80	100	100	50

Mondays

Managers tell us that it is difficult to be truly productive, that is, add much value, on Mondays because these days are filled with the following:

- Catching up on e-mails that have accumulated over the weekend.
- Dealing with small problems that were not resolved the previous week.
- Handling phone calls that were not made on the previous Friday.
- Dealing with "fires" that could not be addressed over the weekend.
- Attending regularly scheduled staff meetings that are not especially value-laden.
- Having trouble getting organized and focused after the weekend.
- Chatting with co-workers about sports and other weekend events.

Tuesdays

Leaders feel that they are beginning to bring value to the business as they improve their focus and are less distracted by routine work. There are often fewer scheduled business meetings held on Tuesdays, which frees up valuable time. If a leader is able to complete a lot of routine work on Monday, he or she can be quite effective on Tuesday.

Wednesdays and Thursdays

These are the high-impact days. Leaders are organized, focused and ready to make a difference in the business. It seems that many of us figure out by Wednesday how to push our business, department or team forward—and we are determined to make this day and Thursday truly productive. Often, important strategy or decision-making meetings or presentations are scheduled on these days.

Fridays

This least productive day of the week results from some obvious and not so obvious factors and conditions. The obvious: people are tired; they need to complete routine work that has accumulated during the week; and they are often dealing with other employees whose focus is on the upcoming weekend.

We have discovered, however, other reasons why Fridays are less productive:

- Many Americans have vacation homes and are leaving the office early to spend the weekend at that second home.
- Traffic in some of the major U.S. metropolitan areas is so intense on Fridays that people leave early to avoid gridlock.
- Government and other offices have instituted flexible schedules whereby employees are off every other Friday, so approvals, contracts, decisions, etc., cannot be completed or advanced.
- Employees are traveling back home from assignments in other locations and are not available for substantive interaction.

Other Work Week Patterns

As you read this chapter, you probably concluded that the typical work week we describe and discuss is one associated with office work. You would be correct. And, clearly, other patterns of personal productivity are all around us: construction sites, medical centers, police departments, and bars and restaurants. In the bar business, for example, Monday may be the slowest day while Friday could be super busy and, if all goes well, very productive and profitable. For leaders in the fields of police, fire fighting and rescue work, any day can be challenging and demanding. It is especially important, we believe, for these leaders to keep a productivity score because there is so much for them to learn from a specific circumstance or event. And being aware of the factors and conditions that led to good outcomes (or bad ones) can be valuable to their ongoing leadership.

Your Turn

Establishing Your Productivity Goals

Now that we have discussed productivity scoring in some detail, we invite you to create a weekly score sheet that you believe is achievable.

Note: For those leaders with irregular schedules, choose a pattern that you would like to have when "all goes well" for you.

Productivity Scores: My Goals

Monday	Tuesday	Wednesday	Thursday	Friday	Saturday	Sunday

Frame 3

Qualitative vs. Quantitative

Qualitative vs Quantitative

You probably recall the definition of leadership that we laid out in the opening chapter: **Leaders must complete ill-defined, qualitative work that adds value to the business.**

What do we mean by "qualitative"? When evaluating leadership effectiveness, it is not how hard a person works or how many hours he or she puts in, it is whether the leader adds value to the business that counts. As we discussed in the opening of this book, leaders normally do not have well-defined roles or responsibilities. To reiterate, leaders don't install GPS systems in cars, don't chop vegetables in a restaurant kitchen, don't drive a truck across country. Their primary responsibility is to make a qualitative contribution to the business—which may involve just a few minutes in a day: analyzing a business process, making an important decision, thinking of new ways to control costs, identifying a new customer or client, deciding whether to hire a new staff member. So, for leaders, it's not necessarily about quantity of time but rather about quality of effort.

Through this framework, we'd like to show that successful leaders find ways to add value regardless of the time and effort needed to do so. Below is a good example:

> *"Our conference center was hosting an evening awards dinner for a national insurance association. Before ending my day, I decided to visit the kitchen, where I saw a worker stacking up a large number of frozen fish filets on a table. Realizing that the kitchen team may have been overpreparing, I asked the chef if he had received word that the association's meeting planner had called. He said, 'No, I haven't been told anything.'*
>
> *The meeting planner had called the resort earlier, reducing the number of attendees at the formal dinner by almost half because bad weather in the Midwest had caused dozens of flight cancellations. After I explained this change to the chef, he leaped into action and directed the food preparation team to recalibrate their efforts. We avoided preparing expensive meals for 85 people. As a result of an interaction—which lasted just five minutes—I made a significant contribution to our business. My productivity score for that day was 100."*

To further illustrate this Qualitative vs. Quantitative framework, we present the following comparisons:

Quantitative:	The sales rep makes 20 customer visits each week.
Qualitative:	The manager teaches the sale rep techniques for advancing the sales process.

Quantitative:	The IT Help Desk team answers 120 inquiries from end-users.
Qualitative:	The IT manager identifies new software that will automate certain elements of the support that the team provides.

Quantitative:	The bakers produce 3000 bagels each morning to meet the 7 a.m. deliveries to retail outlets.
Qualitative:	The VP of Marketing designs new colorful retail packaging, which helps distinguish the company's bagels from its competitors'.

Quantitative:	The hospital lab technicians process 20 blood tests manually per hour.
Qualitative:	The Lab Director streamlines the process required to enter test results into the hospital medical record system.

The point we want to reiterate here is that leaders are the ones who make a qualitative difference in the company or organization. The employees are simply too busy doing the core work, which must be done hour by hour. So, they look to their leaders to identify ways to improve the process, to enhance safety, reduce clean-up time, etc.

Your Turn

Following the pattern above, describe well-defined tasks (quantitative) carried out by the employees under your direction. Then describe your leadership input—technology, process, modifications, improvements, etc., that can add value to your employees' efforts.

Quantitative (team):	
Qualitative (me):	

Quantitative (team):	
Qualitative (me):	

Quantitative (team):	
Qualitative (me):	

Productivity Scoring Helps

When scoring their daily productivity, as we suggested in the last chapter, leaders find that very often just a few minutes in a day make a huge impact on their organization. They realize, for instance, that one very effective ten-minute conversation with a client ends up creating new business that lasts for years. Here's an example:

The director of programs for a training company we consult with was offering a major corporation a 12-hour program in advanced communications skills. The corporation's VP of IT hoped to institute the training in offices all over the country, but could not justify taking systems engineers and technicians out of their offices for two full days. So, the VP said, "Thanks, but no thanks." Two days later, while sitting at his desk, the director thought of a schedule that had not been used by the company before. He then called the VP and explained, "We can offer the training on three mornings, from 8 a.m. to 12 noon, and your systems people will be free to work in the afternoons." The VP thought the idea was excellent—and the training has been held continually for three years. In a few seconds of "qualitative" leadership, the director created a significant revenue stream for his company.

Frame 4

Controlling Routine Work

The Challenge of Routine Work

In Chapter 1, we mentioned that many upper-level managers and executives report low productivity scores, often for weeks on end. During a training session with leaders managing an international health program with staff in ten developing countries, the average scores were unusually low:

Monday	Tuesday	Wednesday	Thursday	Friday
50	40	70	50	40

When asked why there was this uniformity of low scores throughout a group of upper-level managers, they were quick to answer that there was too much routine work and too much time spent traveling.

A national newspaper recently described the work circumstances of the CEO of a health care products corporation. Despite his leadership position, he reported feeling like a prisoner to his calendar. He was discouraged by the fact that he could not spend enough time at medical centers talking to doctors and patients about his company's products. And executives in other fields interviewed by the newspaper talked about the lack of time for serious thinking and face-to-face interactions with important players in their businesses.

We hear this refrain time and again. And what has been most surprising is that the lowest scores often come from leaders at the highest levels of businesses and organizations. We are tempted to call the following a truism: The higher you stand in the organization, the more difficult it is to have high productivity scores.

International Trade Development VP

> *"When I am back in the home office, I have so many phone calls, emails, paperwork and so many reports that are due, along with other small matters to take care of, that sometimes I feel like a clerk—even though I'm a highly paid senior executive. I can't seem to find the time to spend on more important matters. It's not a good situation."*

Because of this phenomenon, we now find ourselves being asked to help companies address the challenge of controlling routine work—which takes us to our next framework.

Adding Value by Controlling Routine Work

The graph below illustrates a somewhat counterintuitive view of adding value:

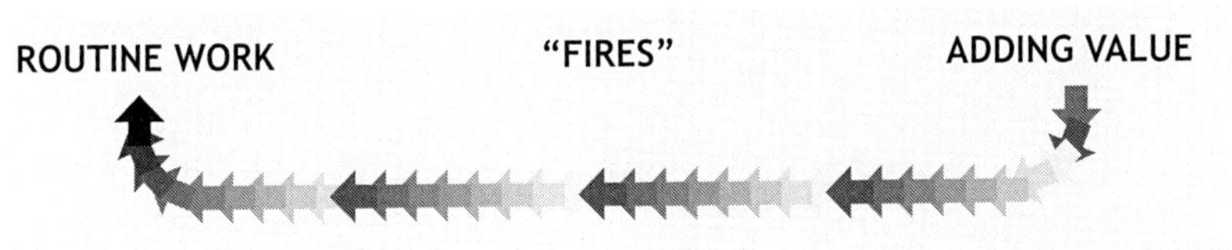

Simply put, one important step you can take to add value in your job is to identify ways of controlling routine work. From our experience with hundreds of departments, divisions, and companies, we have identified five key ways to do so:

Five Steps for Controlling Routine Work

1. Eliminate
2. Automate
3. Reduce
4. Simplify
5. Outsource

EARS and O in Action

In our post-industrial, digital society, leaders are looking at every process in their business, from producing computer chips to renovating houses and checking in airline passengers. The application of technology to business processes is advancing at such a rapid pace that a new book on this topic alone could be published every six months. Consider just these five:

Robots
Drones
Self-propelled equipment and vehicles
Additive manufacturing (i.e., 3D printing)
Cognitive computing

Rather than trying to discuss all of the trends in automation, we'd like to stimulate your ideas with a few modest but typical examples of controlling routine work by leaders who are always on the lookout for time- and resource-saving ideas:

Director, Conference Center Events: Eliminate, Reduce, Simplify

"One morning while sitting in a meeting in a ballroom of one of our hotels, I noticed that not one person at my table poured a glass of water from the pitcher that sat in the middle or our table. The pitcher was attractive, stainless steel, and sat on a small plate with a napkin on top. I thought about how much effort went into filling this pitcher, bringing it to the room, laying it out with the plate and napkin, and later cleaning all three for the next event. And this is repeated thousands of times a month for the tables at conferences, meetings, and training events.

Suddenly, it struck me that we could simply put in the corner of the room a water cooler along with glasses. As it turns out, we did just that, but also added lemon and lime pieces to the transparent, stand-alone container, which gave it a lot of appeal. To make sure these water stations were modern and attractive, we've had to buy expensive ones, but the annual savings has been astounding since we have eliminated pitchers, plates and napkins and all the labor associated with them. And we're talking about two ballrooms and 12 meeting rooms with hundreds of tables, occupied day in and day out over a given year. Surprisingly, we have not yet received one complaint from meeting participants. They don't mind having to stand up and go to the water stations. In fact, we have been praised for a system considered very sanitary and eco-friendly."

President, Insurance Company: Automate, Reduce, Simplify

Whenever a new sales executive joins his insurance firm, Rick has to spend hours explaining the features and subtleties of the various insurance options and more hours advising the new person about the approach the agents take to sales and client service.

But Rick worried about how much the new sales executives were retaining, given that there was so much information to absorb in a short period. So, Rick turned to the digital recorder feature on his smart phone and began recording all of the information, processes and insights that he had previously been explaining in one-on-one meetings with the sales executives. He now emails a digital file to all new executives so they can listen to the information when it's convenient for them—and can listen as many times as they like.

For his part, Rick reduced the stress associated with explaining his business again and again and freed up many hours he was investing in the meetings. Now, once new team members have had an opportunity to listen to a recording a number of times, all Rick has to do is hold a meeting in which he asks questions to ensure that they understand the process well.

Head Chef at a Large Conference Center: Automate, Reduce

"Training and retraining our kitchen staff on plate presentation and special dinner party set-up was wearing me out. So, I turned to my digital pad to reduce my work and improve outcomes. I had one of my chefs photograph all of our plate presentations and all of our set-ups and write out explanations for how everything is done. Now my kitchen team can go right to the computer and review the process each time we have a large group dinner. We are also using the digital material to train new hires, which has freed up even more of my time."

Regional Manager, Office Supply: Simplify, Reduce

As a regional manager in a large office supply retail company, Elizabeth is on the phone for at least five hours a day. She has to speak with the 15 managers she leads, with corporate and regional office staff and with suppliers. To increase the efficiency of these calls, Elizabeth began a process of emailing a series of questions to the other person before each call so that he or she has time to think about the issues or topics to be addressed in the call. As a result, the phone calls are much more focused and efficient. Because the other person has given some thought to the topics, Elizabeth can start the calls quickly and can stay on target by moving from one question to the next. The benefit has been substantial as Elizabeth reduced the total amount of time devoted to daily phone conversations by about 40 percent.

VP, Corporate Acquisitions: Reduce, Eliminate

"As an executive who must travel to evaluate pending business acquisitions for my corporation, I found myself involved with too many routine matters, which kept me glued to my cell phone during every business trip. But I found a solution. I began inviting my senior office administrator, David, to all the important meetings I attend at headquarters so that he would be able to answer inquiries while I'm traveling. He and I also spend additional time discussing some of these issues after the meetings so he has a good grasp of the details. After a couple of months, I sent out an email advising the staff to direct all inquiries to him first. David now does such a good job that my phone calls have dropped 50 percent. And with each meeting he attends and each month that goes by, he becomes even more adept at handling questions, problems, requests, and so forth."

Manager of Maintenance: Outsource, Simplify, Reduce

"Being responsible for the maintenance of a large garden-style rental apartment complex means I have to supervise a large number of staff. One area that was taking up a lot of my time was the landscaping on the property. Realizing how much time I was spending hiring workers, handling and storing the equipment, and dealing with personnel conflicts, etc., I decided to outsource the whole thing. The company we contracted cuts the lawn, trims the shrubs and trees, plants the flowers and in the winter clears the snow-covered roads and pavements. I don't know why I didn't outsource these services before. I now have more time to focus on much more added-value components of the business such as saving energy in all of our buildings."

Your Turn

After taking another look at the five ways of controlling routine work, can you apply one or several to your present work circumstances? We recommend you consider every aspect of your work, such as reporting, auditing, communication, meetings, presentations, approvals, phone calls and conference calls.

EARS and O

1. ____________________

2. ____________________

3. ____________________

4. ____________________

5. ____________________

Controlling Routine through Appropriate Assertiveness

We would be remiss if we leave this discussion of getting a grip on routine work without discussing one of the fundamental behaviors—assertiveness—that lies beneath some, if not all, of the steps we are suggesting you take.

As the following examples illustrate, a leader sometimes has no choice but to be assertive in order to gain control over his or her routine work. This assertiveness is not easy for many leaders who, in their careers, moved up by saying "yes" and by taking on more work when asked to do so. At some point, however, saying yes can be counter-productive.

After you review the two examples of assertiveness, we'll ask you to apply this approach to your situation.

Director, Office of Security

> Patrick's job is to oversee the security of a large corporate campus, in which there are hundreds of rooms involving 20 levels of access. Eight of the areas are designated "highest security."
>
> For 12 years, Patrick had done a good job of maintaining tight security and avoiding theft of information. During March, a security auditor arrived from the international HQs to conduct an audit of the entire building. The auditor scored the facility at the highest level but still made several recommendations, the most substantial of which was that Patrick should start producing a weekly report on entry to the eight code-red areas, which would be sent to two high-level administrators in the corporate office.
>
> Patrick decided to be frank with the auditor: "I want you to know that I review the entry report for these areas every week myself. And every month I send a report of all entries to the Exec VP here in the building. She has told me on several occasions that she does not have the time to review them."
>
> "Therefore, I feel I must ask you two questions: Why create such a report if the officers at HQs have not asked for it? And

what leads you to believe that the reports will improve security?" The auditor agreed that he could not say exactly how the report would improve security. After further discussion with Patrick, he deleted the request from his final report.

Because Patrick asserted himself, he succeeded in preventing an unnecessary increase in his routine work.

Director of Business Development

"My productivity was being seriously undermined by all of the conference calls the company requires me to be part of. Some days, I would participate in five separate calls—some lasting over two hours. One day, I decided to assert myself with my boss and went to her office with a suggestion. 'Why don't you have the various teams place me first on any meeting agenda they develop? And if they don't have an agenda, let me be the first presenter. In this way, I can finish in 15 to 20 minutes and get back to my other work.' I was pleasantly surprised that she agreed. With this one change, I have gained nearly two hours a day of productive work time."

Regional Director of IT

"Since I am responsible for small computer systems improvement projects all over the country, my company has me meet in person with each of the project directors four times a year. Though it's a good idea to do the visits, I end up spending so much time traveling that I can't invest a lot of time in client relations, which is important to our company's future. Fortunately, on a recent visit to the field, one of the directors noticed that I looked a bit frazzled and suggested that I use videoconferencing. It only took me a second to realize how good her idea was. Now I do two of the four yearly meetings by videoconferencing and have cut my travel in half. And the video quality is so good these days that I feel like the directors and I are meeting in person. I should have started doing this a long time ago!"

Your Turn

Can you identify three or four routine tasks or responsibilities you could automate, eliminate, reduce or simplify if you "pushed back," that is, asserted your needs.

1. ____

2. ____

3. ____

4. ____

Finally, as you continue to identify ways to control routine work, keep in mind that whatever time and energy you free up positions you to make a qualitative difference in your business.

Frame 5

Skill and Will

Playing the Four Roles of Leadership

Although most leaders have an instinctual sense of which employees are strong performers and which are not, it is important to have a framework for thinking systematically—and, therefore, more deeply—about your team. To this end, we developed a simple but powerful framework for analyzing employees and your leadership role with them. This framework consists of two critical categories, *skill* and *will*, which, in turn, create four distinct groups of employees. From this grouping, it will be apparent that you are asked to play four distinct roles, all in response to the attitude and capacity of your team members.

Skill and Will: Four Categories of Management and Leadership

Group	Skill	Will	Description	Your Role
1	10 9	10 9	Self-starting, mature, independent, productive	Lead only
2	5 4	10 9	Eager, energetic, inexperienced, dependent	Develop, mentor
3	7 6	7 7	Dependable, reactive, not ambitious	Manage
4	5 9	5 3	Undependable, immature, high maintenance	Supervise, caretake

(Scale: 1-10 with 10 the highest)

Our Terminology

We use the term *skill* in the traditional sense: Does the person possess the skill set needed to do the job? Is the person proficient? If you have a lab technician who completes lab tests correctly and consistently, that person may be a 9 or 10. A new lab technician who is learning the procedures of your lab might be rated as a 6. If there is a lab technician who has experience but through lack of good concentration skills makes mistakes regularly and causes lab work to be redone, that person might be rated as a 4. And so on.

The term *will* is more subjective. Is the employee positive, enthusiastic, energetic, fully engaged and motivated to do what it takes to get the job done and ready to make an extra effort when required? That employee would be rated a 9 or 10. Other employees are motivated and energetic only on certain days or when doing certain tasks that appeal to them. Those employees would be rated as a 6 or 7. And so on.

Value of This Framework

As we mentioned above, after rating employees on their *skill* and *will*, you'll quickly see that, as a leader, you have not one but four separate roles to play—depending especially on the *will* of the person you manage and/or lead.

Group 1: High Skill & High Will

These are the wonderful people who make your organization successful. They know the work, do it right without cajoling, and have a sense of urgency about completing their assignments. And since their *will* is so high, they consistently produce high-quality outcomes, be it a product or service. They are, in effect, more your business partners than your employees.

> *"Whenever one of us in the finance office faces a tough problem or decision, we turn to Vanessa because she will do whatever she can to help—and does it pleasantly. Since she has so much experience, she usually comes up with the best approach. It's hard to think what my team and I would do if she were not here."*

> *"Tom is so independent and competent that I sometimes forget to talk to him about his department, which is the second largest in my division. Everyone who works for him respects him, and as a result, his team meets their deadlines month in and month out. I know if there is something for me to be concerned about, Tom will tell me right away. Because of the confidence I have in him, I can spend much more time working with the other departments."*

> *"Having Maria Elena working for me is heaven. She keeps her ten sales team members motivated and energized. She's constantly working closely with them, taking some of the administrative load off their shoulders and teaching them advanced selling techniques. She's so effective that no one has turned over in her department in two years. And the clients love her, not just because she is so warm and personable but because she knows the business inside and out. I just try to stay out of her way so I don't interfere with her success."*

Your role with *high-skill/high-will* employees, be they managers or hourly employees, is to lead them. These self-starters do not need to be managed. In fact, managing them may reduce their will to succeed. These are folks who are self-motivated, self-directed and who have very high standards. When there is a problem, they will come to you. When they need help, they will ask you. In general terms, your leadership role is to appreciate their efforts, ask them how you can be of assistance, and make certain they have the resources they need. Later in this chapter, we'll make specific suggestions for supporting these superb performers.

Group 2: Low Skill & High Will

A new hire is a good example of an employee who falls into this category. It could be a young person coming into the world of business for the first time or a woman who after raising children has decided to return to the workplace. Since, like those in Category #1, they are *high-will*, they do not need to be managed so much as trained and developed. And your efforts to develop them will pay off since they not only have a good attitude but also enthusiasm and an openness to input from others. It can be a real pleasure to lead and work with these employees as you develop them to become members of Group 1.

Group 3: Medium Skill & Medium Will

This group includes what is commonly referred to as the "average employee," which may not really be a fair assessment of them. These are often solid performers who simply require more investment of your time and energy than do Groups 1 and 2. They will get the job done if provided clear direction and regular follow-up by their manager or leader. Often, these are employees who come to work primarily to earn a living and are not focused on advancing along a career path. They often have a second job or a source of life satisfaction unrelated to career.

> *"I have 20 assemblers who must work hard each day to keep up with our workload. If I work closely with them, they get the job done. But I can't be away from the work area for extended periods or they back off from the work a bit. They're all good people, but they are here mostly to get a paycheck. Managing them takes up a lot of my time, but by doing so, I know that at the end of the day we will meet our production goals."*

If this group is managed well, the results can be very good. But a hands-off approach can lead to problems. All of the traditional management skills you have learned must be applied here: delegation, follow-up, monitoring of performance, coaching to enhance skill development, and so forth.

Group 4: Low Will

This last group is, without question, the most challenging to describe and to deal with. Note that in the title of the category above, we do not mention *skill* level—which is irrelevant because these employees have no real desire to do the work or play the role that has been assigned to them. With a *will* level of 5 or below, these employees cannot be trusted to do their work or to do it well, regardless of their level of *skill* or the number of years of experience. They need constant monitoring and the closest supervision possible. Even then, the results may be disappointing.

> *"When I took over my department, I inherited a market analyst who has no real interest in her work and who can't seem to write more than one or two decent reports a month. And when I try to coach her, she gives me all kinds of excuses and blames other people on the team for her troubles. When meeting with her, I feel as if nothing I say has any effect. What bothers me most is how she bad-mouths the company to the new analysts and to our admin people. I don't know what to do with her."*

There is no easy answer to how a leader should deal with employees in this group. We often hear the refrain, "I have to baby-sit the person day in and day out." Accordingly, most companies encourage their leaders to "move these employees up or out," that is, help them increase their *will* or help them leave the company.

The Full Range of Ratings (Scores)

Before we invite you to rate your employees, we would like to clarify the rating system, though it is probably already obvious to you. The sample scores we presented above do not, of course, cover the full spectrum. To prevent any confusion, we list all the possible ratings or scores in the chart that follows:

Skill vs. Will:

Four Categories of Management and Leadership

Skill	Will	Description	Your Role
GROUP 1			
10	10	Self-starting, mature, independent, productive	Lead Only
10	9		
9	10		
9	9		
9	8		
8	9		
8	8		
GROUP 2			
7	10	Eager, energetic, inexperienced	Develop, mentor
6	10		
5	10		
4	10		
3	10		
2	10		
1	10		
7	9		
6	9		
5	9		
4	9		
3	9		
2	9		
1	9		
7	8		
6	8		
5	8		
4	8		
3	8		
2	8		
1	8		

Skill	Will	Description	Your Role
		GROUP 3	
7	7	Dependable, reactive, not ambitious	Manage
6	7		
7	6		
6	6		
		GROUP 4	
10	5	Undependable, immature	Supervise, caretake
10	4		
10	3		
10	2		
10	1		
9	5		
9	4		
9	3		
9	2		
9	1		
8	5		
8	4		
8	3		
8	2		
8	1		
…	…		
1	1		

Notes:

In Group 2, the *skill* level rating can vary from 1 to 10. The critical rating, though, is the *will*, which must be 8 or above.

In Group 4, the *skill* level rating, again, can vary from 1 to 10. The critical score is the *will*, which must be 5 or below.

Clearly, some of these scores are not seen in the real world (e.g., 1 10 or 10 1), but we wanted to give you the complete scoring scale.

Your Turn

Using our framework, rate your employees (or a reasonable number of them) below. If you have only a few employees who report directly to you, consider scoring staff in other departments or divisions with which you work.

Employee	Skill Level	Will Level

Strategizing for Leading the Four Groups of Employees

Now that you have rated your team, we encourage you to develop a strategy, based on levels of *skill* and *will*, for each of the four groups. Let's begin with the highest performers.

Group 1: Leading High-Skill/High-Will Employees

Since these are the best of the best, they can be called on for new ideas, for better ways of doing the work, for discussing with you important issues in the business. As mentioned earlier, a good starting point for your leadership role is to view these employees as business partners. And out of this stance flow certain strategies, such as the following:

> *"If Jackie has an opening in her busy schedule, I invite her to join me for meetings with our suppliers. This gives her a chance to understand the business more deeply and to learn how to manage these relationships. Often, I turn to her in these meetings for her thoughts on the problems we are wrestling with. Because Jackie is such a mature, responsible person, I may be able to turn this responsibility over to her, which will be a big plus for me as I will then have more open time in my schedule."*

Besides inviting *high-skill, high-will* employees to join you for important meetings and events, you can have them represent you at meetings in which others seek the prospective of your department or division. Below are a number of other possibilities leaders have told us are good for the employee and good for the company:

- Ask them to oversee the development of Group 2 employees.
- Have them take responsibility for developing important presentations (to executives, clients, owners), allowing them to do some of the interviews and information gathering that is required.
- Recommend them for a corporate task force, which will expose them to other aspects of the business.
- Send them to industry trade shows, exhibitions, and conferences and ask them to make a presentation to your division or department about what they observed and what they learned.

We would be remiss if we ended this discussion without emphasizing that we have a responsibility to ensure that the needs of these wonderful employees are met. In this way, they will be retained—often for many years. However, from our experience, if *high-will, high-skill* employees are asked, "What can I or the company do for you?" they will often respond stoically, telling you that all is well even when it's not. As the following vignette reminds us, we must make a continuous effort to find out what these employees want and need, or we may miss an opportunity to provide them the support they deserve.

> Alexandra, the senior manager in a large event planning company, had planned a trip from her East Coast location to San Diego, where she would spend Christmas and a few days after with her parents and other family members. Since the company was managing a very lucrative and high-profile evening of events on New Year's Eve, she planned to return on the evening of December 30 to ensure that all went well.
>
> A couple of weeks before her trip, her boss, the Chief Operating Officer, had scheduled time to ask Alexandra about work and her team. Near the end of the conversation, he asked about her upcoming trip and learned that her family was arriving in San Diego from various cities around the country and included uncles, aunts and cousins whom she had not seen in years. The COO wondered aloud why she was not planning to stay in San Diego for a longer period of time. Alexandra explained that she felt she had to return so she could oversee the New Year's Eve events.
>
> The manager immediately committed to finding another person to fill in for her and urged her to remain longer with her family and friends. Because of that conversation, Alexandra stayed five extra days, had a great time with her family and returned to the office in high spirits.

The manager's productivity score for this day should be 100. Even though the conversation entailed only about 20 minutes of his time, he made a qualitative contribution to the business by supporting an outstanding employee. He was able to add value because he did the following:

- Set aside time to ask about her work and her plans and took the time to find out important details of her trip.
- Had the wisdom to ask a question that revealed how he could be of help to her.
- Quickly agreed to make adjustments for her sake.
- Encouraged her to invest in her personal well-being.
- Made the offer with no strings attached.

As this vignette illustrates, it may take some of your highest level communication skills to ensure that the organization is, indeed, meeting the needs of Group 1 employees, who may be managers, supervisors or line staff. There are many good reasons why we end up taking these valuable people for granted:

> *"Christine is so good that I sometimes forget that I am supposed to be leading her. Maybe, in all honesty, it is because she is so strong and competent I always leave her alone to do what she needs to do."*

Alexandra, Christine and other *high-skill, high-will* people like them usually do not crave attention—and as we mentioned, they may even be stoical, taking whatever confronts them without complaint. Therefore, we recommend that you establish a habit of checking in with them from time to time, asking them key questions that show you value their work and input. Below are three areas to focus on:

- **After reviewing your high-will performers' list of added-value tasks, actions, initiatives, etc., pose a series of questions in an effort to determine if you can be of help to them.**

> *"Have you been able to find time to meet with software vendors about developing a new approach for us?"*

> *"What do you think about costs now that you know more about the company's initiative?"*

- **Inquire about their team and their team's productivity.**

  "Are you able to leave Andy on his own now or does he still need close supervision?"

  "How well is Rebecca fitting in with the team?"

- **Ask what you can do for them.**

  "We once discussed your working out of your home once a week. Would you like me to look into that possibility with my higher-ups?"

  "Is there anything I can do to reduce your workload, which I realize has gotten heavy lately?"

  It's particularly important that you ask this last question since these highly motivated people will often keep working hard no matter what personal sacrifice is required of them.

Your Turn

Create a list of questions that would help you to give quality attention to one of your Group 1 staff. Consider following the above pattern, asking about their added-value efforts, their team, and their personal needs.

1. ______________________________

2. ______________________________

3. ______________________________

4. ______________________________

5. ______________________________

6. ______________________________

Group 2: Developing and Mentoring Low-Skill/High-Will Employees

As discussed earlier, your role is to mentor and develop these motivated employees. Leaders tell us that they work hard to build the skills of this group so that they do not become bored or lose their momentum. When possible, recruit a Group 1 person to oversee their development. Working closely with, or shadowing, a *high-skill, high-will* performer can get this "green" employee focused on quality and productivity early in his or her tenure.

> *"I feel bad some days when I see Aaron walking up to other staff and asking if he can help them with their work. The fellow wants so much to be productive that he'll help anybody with anything. The problem is that my team is making decisions about portfolios that require a lot of experience. What I may do is assign him to work with one of our senior analysts, Megan, who, because she may retire next year, is overseeing some of our smaller accounts. The hands-on experience with a pro like Megan should set Aaron up well to fill that slot. Aaron needs our time and support, but the investment is well worth it. He is so positive and eager to learn that he injects energy into our whole office."*

These Group 2 employees are invaluable in the way described above. Because they are enjoyable to have in the office and because they bring a fresh enthusiasm to the enterprise, they make it a better place to work. But they require a leader to carry out a balancing act: providing them development and mentoring but also finding regular productive work that they can do while they are learning. We strongly recommend that you identify both areas (real work and development) before you bring them on board. A helpful approach to the final selection interview could be:

> *"While you're learning how to carry out the client support role you will eventually play, we will be giving you some fairly mundane tasks to complete. In this way, you will be helping the team be more productive while you are learning the business. We hope you'll be patient with us so that you can become one of our lead support specialists in about a year."*

And if these are young people relatively new to the workplace, leaders should be prepared to adjust to their needs. Many of these people will want to work very hard from 8 a.m. to 6 p.m., but leave work on time so that they can go to a fitness center or meet other personal commitments. Since their *will* is often a 9 or 10, it is in the company's interests to be flexible, for they will soon be highly productive and trustworthy staff members.

Group 3: Managing Medium-Skill, Medium-Will Employees

When well managed, this group can be very productive. They will not have the enthusiasm of Group 2 nor the high productivity and resourcefulness of Group 1, but these employees are critical players in most companies since they complete core, well-defined tasks. Fortunately, most people in this category are quite willing to put in a full day's work and do a good job. But they expect to be given very clear directions, a well-organized workplace, and the right equipment and other resources. In short, they expect to be managed professionally.

So a leader (or his or her representative) must invest time and energy in managing this group. And things cannot be left to chance. Consider this scenario at a huge shopping mall construction site:

The Last Hour of the Workday

> A construction consultant was called to the site to help improve the productivity of the crafts (e.g., iron workers, carpenters, welders). Data showed that the construction company was getting the least amount of productivity in the last hour of the day shift. After questioning the site leadership, it was found that the craft superintendents were holding a 20-minute meeting at 3 p.m. each day. But it took the superintendents 10 minutes to walk from their work area to the administration trailer for the meeting and another 10 to return to their work area. In all, they were away from their teams from 2:50 p.m. to 3:30 p.m. Since quitting time for the crafts was at 3:45 p.m., the superintendents were arriving back from the meeting just in time to help everyone clean up and go home.

> Although the crafts were responsible, hard-working people, they tended to finish the tasks they were doing and then wait for the boss to return from the meeting before doing anything else. Once the superintendents rescheduled their meeting to 4 p.m., after the craft had departed, they were able to manage their teams closely in the last hour. And craft productivity rose sharply.

The above scenario lays out the importance of applying traditional management skills (e.g., delegation, follow-up, monitoring of performance, coaching, quality control) so that Group 3 employees can perform at their highest level.

Of course, a number of those in Group 3 will strive to move into Group 2 or Group 1, that is, to become a 7 10, an 8 8 or even a 10 10.

> *"I don't know what happened to Charlene. For four years, she was a pleasant, not particularly ambitious young woman, who did her job in the office and went home. I respected that and never complained about the fact that she wouldn't stay late or take on additional duties. She was a solid performer, and that was fine with me. A few months ago, she came into my office and asked me what it would take for her to move up in the department. I explained that she would have to complete certain training courses, both in-house and on line—and that some of the training would end up being done on her own time.*
>
> *She's now in the middle of the training and doing quite well. Both her attitude and her energy level are much improved, so I think she may end up becoming one of our best performers."*

There are many reasons why a Group 3 employee may suddenly catch fire and increase his or her *will*: recently married; first child arriving; a new boss; a desire to buy a home; or a natural maturing that comes with age. As leaders, our responsibility is to be open to this possibility and respond positively when the employee is ready to improve.

Supporting Group 3

Realizing that Group 3 employees can be engaged and productive, leaders search for ways to create the best workplace circumstances. Sometimes relatively simple actions can facilitate better performance:

For example, a regional operations director for a large hazardous waste recycling company manages a series of field teams who support and service clients in a ten-state area of the U.S. Southeast. He asked us for our help because his team was struggling to explain to their clients the complex regulatory processes that must be followed by all parties involved in the disposal of waste.

Together, we developed responses to the 20 most frequently asked questions (FAQs) by clients. The field technicians were asked to study the responses for just 15 minutes a day and then practice answering the questions out loud with a fellow technician. The effort paid off. The technicians became more confident and more comfortable in front of clients. They also appreciated the increased respect they received from clients, which resulted from the fact that the technicians could discuss the business more easily and in more detail.

As illustrated above, leaders should continually focus on strategies for providing support to Group 3 employees. Although it requires substantial effort, the results can be quite positive.

Group 4: Supervising Low-Will Employees

Any discussion of *low-will* employees is painful. The situation is bad for them and bad for the organization in which they work.

> *"At the meeting of our executive committee, we had scheduled five hours to develop a first draft of our annual business plan. Thirty minutes into the meeting, the group started talking about one supervisor who was not only underperforming but was creating a lot of tension in her department. During the discussion, the group decided to rate her skill and will, which turned out to be 6/4. The team spent 40 minutes of valuable time that was supposed to be devoted to planning and goal setting discussing this one supervisor, how she was hurting the business and why it was difficult to move her out of the company. It was a very frustrating conversation."*

The fact that these executives and upper-level managers felt compelled to invest so much time in discussing one supervisor in a company with hundreds of employees illustrates how disruptive a *low-will* employee can be.

But how or why does an adult become a *low-will* performer? This is one of the most frequently asked questions in our leadership programs. Because *low-will* people seldom volunteer an accurate explanation for their unhappiness or disaffection, it is difficult to answer this question. Although it's mostly guesswork, from our experience, we conclude that there are several common causes of employee *low will*:

- In the wrong job
- Burned out
- Serious unresolved personal problems
- Frustrated by lack of success but blaming others for it
- Immature personality and not ready to commit to career
- A chronically unhappy person who brings that person to work
- Very high expectations (career advancement, salary, interesting work), which the organization cannot meet

The list could go on and on. But such explanations are more the purview of those with professional training in human behavioral issues (e.g., clinical psychologists). As leaders, our responsibility is to offer them help through the company's employee support program (usually offered by Human Resources), show the person how to perform better on the job or remove them from the company. We want to again emphasize that a leader's primary responsibility is to protect the interests and well-being of the customer or client and of those employees who are committed and responsible, and of the organization itself. It is not wise to allow *low-will* employees to undermine any of the aforementioned groups.

> *"I have had to speak to one of my night shift nurses, Miriam, two or three times over the past month. Patients complain that she is impatient and abrupt with them. They feel that she's always in a bad mood. Her impatience is a real problem because she doesn't give good answers to the questions raised with her. She seems to say whatever's on the top of her head and moves*

on. One patient told me that he complained when the alarm on his infusion machine beeped for more than 10 minutes and no one came in to fix the problem. When he complained to Miriam, she said, 'Sir, this is a hospital, not a hotel.'

After speaking with Miriam, I'm concerned she's burned out with nursing. She sees it as just a job and the patient as a pain in the neck. I've asked her to think about what other jobs in the medical center she can apply for. I'll help her do that. But if her behavior continues, I'll have no choice but to continue writing her up and eventually letting her go."

To describe it succinctly, your role with Group 4 employees is to follow the performance management process established at your company (e.g., coaching sessions, verbal warnings, written warnings) and if the person does not show significant improvement, let him or her go from the company.

Note: Clearly, there are exceptions to the above approach. For example, when someone experiences a tragedy in his or her family, the overwhelming majority of organizations do everything possible to make adjustments, even when the person's performance is weak for a substantial period of time. The same applies to serious illness. We have seen, first-hand, dozens of times how companies make sacrifices to adjust to people facing a very serious personal life challenge.

Managing Low-Will Performers

In support of this process, we would like to pass on a few recommendations for dealing with *low-will* employees made by leaders with whom we have worked:

- Begin coaching and counseling the person as soon as the behavior exhibits itself. Do not wait. Though you hope the problem will go away, it probably won't.

"I kept thinking Eric would shape up. He has a lot of talent and knows the business as well as anyone. But he never stopped criticizing other staff out loud or accusing other people of making his life difficult. By the time I realized that he was not going to 'play well with others,' he had been with us six months. He

never admitted to having any responsibility for his poor working relationships. We had to spend quite a bit of money to convince him to leave because I had not documented any of his disruptive behavior."

- As soon as it becomes clear that the *low-will* person is not going to change sufficiently (and you have begun serious documentation), be proactive and offer to help the person search for another job. You can give them one or two days a week to search, even provide them coaching in identifying what industry and what job may fit them better than the one they are presently in. Though this approach can be costly, it is generous—and may help avoid a lawsuit or other disruption in your organization.

- Establish a firm time period by which the employee must improve to the standard you have set during your discussions. Most leaders recommend 8 to 12 weeks.

- If, while you are trying to resolve a performance problem, the person is disruptive to you or others, place him or her in a position where daily interaction with other staff and with customers is minimized.

An Elixir

From our experience, most leaders find it quite difficult to confront a *low-will* person, especially if that person has a strong personality or is strongly resistant to reasonable feedback. We believe we can provide you an elixir that will "steel" your determination to do what is right and performance manage the person with a sense of urgency: Think fairness.

Leaders have an ethical responsibility to create as much fairness in the workplace as possible. *Low-will* employees create unfairness. When they are openly negative or pessimistic, they undermine the morale of others; when they avoid completing their work or do a poor job, they cause someone else to work harder; when they are uncooperative or unsupportive of the organization's goals, they undermine the sense of team; and when they are unpleasant, abrupt or indifferent to customers, they undermine the business on which all other employees are depending for their livelihood. If you focus on the fact that your customers and your employees deserve fairness, it will be much easier for you to become impatient with the poor performance of a *low-will* person.

Again, we do not want to give the impression that carrying out this responsibility is easy.

> *"I have been putting off delivering this performance appraisal to David because I know that it is going to go badly. He becomes defensive whenever you point out any mistake he makes or any weak product he produces. He is difficult to deal with on the best of days. In fact, I'm quite sure he will lodge a complaint with Human Resources against me as soon as he gets the review. This whole matter's been weighing on me for weeks."*

This leader is burning a lot of fuel simply because he knows that this *low-will* employee will not accept deserved negative input maturely or professionally. Obviously, then, documentation is vital since, without it, a leader is in a very difficult position when delivering a tough, negative message to such a *low-will* employee.

The 90-Day Rule

In many states and jurisdictions, there is a 90-day rule relating to new hires. A company can terminate a new employee within that 90-day window without cause. It's considered a trial period, enabling the employer and employee to get a sense of one another.

Every leader should make use of these 90 days to ensure that the organization does not end up with a *low-will* employee.

> *"In our division, the leadership team meets to review every new employee after they have been with us for 60 days. In most cases, managers and supervisors are able to make a decision about the employee's will level within that time. To protect the interests of the new employee, we gather input from three or four managers who work with the person so that the input is not too narrow and possibly biased. If the employee is rated below an 8 in will, we let them go. In our view, an employee, when new, should be very enthusiastic and energetic, trying to make the best impression on his or her peers and bosses. So we do not consider even a rating of 7 in will as adequate."*

Note that the leader speaking above does not mention skill level. She told us that the company is prepared to invest heavily in building the skills of a new employee who is *high-will* because they are almost always anxious to learn and develop.

If the 90-day rule applies to your organization, we recommend that you take advantage of this window to avoid ending up with employees who could cause a great deal of trouble after their employment becomes officially permanent.

Your Turn

We invite you to write out some strategies that you can apply to your management and leadership of the four groups of employees we have been discussing. To help you get started, we again provide you the terminology we have applied to each group:

- Group 1: Lead
- Group 2: Develop, mentor
- Group 3: Manage
- Group 4: Supervise, "handhold"

My strategies with Group 1:

1.

2.

3.

4.

My strategies with Group 2:

1. ____________________

2. ____________________

3. ____________________

4. ____________________

My strategies with Group 3:

1. ____________________

2. ____________________

3. ____________________

4. ____________________

My strategies with Group 4:

1. ____________________

2. ____________________

3. ____________________

4. ____________________

Hire For Will

If a position does not require a technical background and specialized knowledge, most leaders tell us that they will hire for *will* and not for *skill.* Finding a person with both *high-skill* and *high-will* is clearly the first choice. But there are many positions in the world of business and industry that allow for learning on the job. Some are technical but do not require extensive technical training. In these cases, most leaders would rather hire a *high-will* person whose skills are not fully developed, realizing that such a person will be cooperative, proactive and supportive of other staff.

After all, you may have to live with this person for years to come. Therefore, you want to hire a person you'd like to see every day and one who makes you glad you are his or her leader—a circumstance that results from hiring for *high will.*

Frame 6

Efficiency vs. Effectiveness

Choosing Efficiency or Effectiveness

The fact that leadership is more art than science becomes even more obvious when we apply the framework of *efficiency* vs. *effectiveness*. A leader is frequently deciding—often unconsciously—whether to be efficient or effective in any task or interaction.

Choosing Efficiency

> *"Bill, I really want to hear the details of how you and your team handled the client's resistance to our price increase, but I have to catch a 4:50 flight. Could you just send me the fixed price structure for next year in an email so I can give that data to my bosses?"*

Choosing Effectiveness

> *"Why don't you and Joyce put aside what you're doing this morning and explain in detail to me why you think we should hire more support staff. And I'll clear my calendar so we can figure out what to do."*

Of course, each of us is continually making decisions within this framework in our personal lives. For example, if we are hungry but in a hurry, we microwave a frozen dinner. This choice is very efficient but, as we all know, it comes with some cost in nutrition and taste. If we have the time and energy, we cook a meal from scratch using fresh ingredients (effective) and accept the tradeoff of time and energy for good taste and nutrition. Below are some other examples illustrating how we make hard choices about being efficient or effective.

Efficient		Effective
Drive to the store	vs.	Bike or walk to the store
Send an e-mail	vs.	Visit someone in person
Hire someone to do it	vs.	Do it yourself
See the movie	vs.	Read the book

In the workplace, a savvy leader is aware of when she chooses *efficiency* and when she chooses *effectiveness*—and realizes that each choice has consequences.

> *"My boss Eva is a very hard-working woman who is clearly dedicated to her job and work. Unfortunately, she is almost always in a rush and does not take the time to explain the whys and the wherefores behind projects that we, the staff, are asked to complete. It is difficult for us to make decisions sometimes because we are not clear about the purpose of the project. This often results in delays while we wait for Eva to make decisions. Eva may think that her efficiency is saving the division money, but, in fact, in the longer term, it reduces the productivity of everyone around her."*

Now, to be fair to Eva, she is clearly very hard-working and likely a serious *high-will* professional who is trying to do her best all the time. The words, "Unfortunately, she is almost always in a rush," indicate that she simply has too much work to do and therefore turns to efficient interactions with her staff—interactions that lead to decisions not being made and projects being delayed.

If we were asked to coach Eva, we would recommend that she focus on our five steps for controlling routine work. With a focused effort, Eva can probably find a way to reduce her workload or delegate more, even if she cannot find a way to eliminate or automate it. We find that many talented, highly motivated managers and executives have trouble delegating work because they suffer from the perfectionist's mantra: "If I do it, I know it will be done right." Moreover, they can't reduce or simplify their work because they lack the free time to strategize in this direction. So, they simply soldier on, hoping one day they'll catch up and have time to breathe, think, etc. Sadly, that time often does not come. But some leaders find time to be effective, no matter what:

> *"Even though the general manager of our resort hotel is a very busy man dealing with the hotel owners, the regional corporate office and all of the problems that arise at the hotel, he manages to hold a two-hour sales strategy meeting with the entire sales team every week. Before that meeting, he spends a couple of hours analyzing sales data and trends and then works with me to develop a detailed agenda so that the meeting is focused and hard hitting. He has admitted to me that it is difficult to find the*

three or four hours a week he must invest in this process, but the pay-off has been significant. Our sales are ahead of last year by almost 8 percent."

In the above vignette, the general manager has to struggle to find the time to analyze sales data and to meet with his team. To find time for this effective effort, he probably has to make some hard choices about what work to set aside. He may even have to ask for forgiveness from his bosses on the regional team for deadlines he misses. But as a leader preoccupied with adding value, he knows that driving sales stands above almost all his other responsibilities and is therefore willing to takes risks to be effective and make such sales happen.

Let's now turn to a few standard or recurring responsibilities that can require us to decide whether to be efficient or effective. Since meetings are such a huge part of a leader's work these days, we'll start with them:

Meetings

For reasons that are not entirely clear to us, the overwhelming majority of managers and leaders we work with tell us that they do not like to attend meetings. Their distaste for meetings is so strong that they don't even break their meetings down into those that are valuable and those that are not. They just say that they don't like meetings. Most likely, the reason for this strong distaste is that so many meetings do not add value. Here's what we believe happens: To save time, leaders decide to make their meetings as efficient as possible and simply talk at the team as they sit in a room.

We call these "information transfer" meetings. We all know how these meetings go: One person "tells" and everyone else sits and listens. Often, there are few or no questions asked and then everyone goes back to work. Now, there are times when such efficient meetings need to be held. For example, there's been a change in the business or a recent decision that affects everyone and their work:

"Good news, everyone. The equity partner that we have been in negotiations with has decided to invest significantly in our company. As you can imagine, this will lead to changes in our operations, both here and overseas. Though you'll receive

details of the deal by the end of the week, for now we'd like you to know that Headquarters will remain here in Houston and no one working here will have to relocate as a result of this new partnership."

In this instance, the Vice President of Finance wants to tell the team as quickly as possible the good news that the deal is done and that no one has to relocate.

But we strongly suggest that leaders avoid, whenever possible, holding these meetings. Instead, the leader can send this straightforward information either in an email or in a digital recording that can be easily emailed to every employee. The problem isn't just that employees feel that meetings are of little value, but also that having to attend a meeting can break the productive rhythm of a person's day. If they are in the middle of completing a calculation, writing a report, reviewing a proposal, gathering information for a client or customer, they suddenly have to stop what they're doing, leave their work area and go to the meeting room. When they return to their desk, it can be difficult to refocus on the work they were doing.

Clearly, then, leaders should keep the number of "information transfer" meetings to a minimum. All of which leads us to the question, "What are effective meetings?"

We consider meetings to be effective when:

- Topics, issues or challenges are analyzed and discussed.
- Decisions have to be made—or at least clarified.
- New ideas are being sought (practical creative thinking by the group).
- Disagreements, tensions, or conflicts have to be worked out.
- Individuals or teams are given recognition and there's some celebration.

Prepping for Meetings

To greatly increase the likelihood that an effective meeting will add value for you and your team, there's no substitute for meeting preparation. The first step, obviously, is to create an agenda, especially one that results from input from colleagues who will be in the meeting.

The second step is to send out the agenda to the participants ahead of time, asking them to make notes and develop questions that the agenda items raise. One nice benefit to this approach is that you can have a "fast start" to the meeting. That is, you can jump right into the first topic and get the discussion moving immediately. For example,

> *"Irma, what questions do you have about our idea of finding a new vendor for our automated customer check-out terminals, which is the first item on our agenda today?"*

> *"David, how are things progressing on the report to the client, which is the first topic we want to discuss this morning?"*

Note: Ironically, having participants arrive with notes and questions and starting your meeting "fast" is an example of injecting efficiency into a meeting that is effective.

Besides the above, other typical steps in meeting preparation are:

- Research
- Data collection
- Interviews
- Careful review of previous meeting notes
- Input and advice from other departments or divisions

As part of our work, we, your authors, are asked to facilitate a significant number of meetings each year. We have found that it is unusually valuable to carry out interviews before any important meeting, not just because we receive lots of good input but also because we avoid carrying our own biases too forcefully into the meeting itself. The interviews enable us to go into the meeting with many thoughts and ideas from others, which, in turn, leaves us more open to the participants' suggestions, input, disagreements, etc.

Above all else, consider doing at least some preparation for any meeting that you believe is important to your work. Even a little preparation can make a big difference.

One-on-One Encounters

Another recurring responsibility that requires us to choose efficiency or effectiveness centers on the one-on-one encounters we have each day.

By effective in this situation we mean that you focus sharply on the other person as he or she talks to you; it means encouraging the person to elaborate and it means asking questions which allow the whole story to be told. For an employee, such interactions are very satisfying and much appreciated. The person feels heard, respected and valued.

But let's be realistic: A leader cannot be effective in every one-on-one conversation that occurs in a work day or he or she would not only become exhausted but would not be able to get all the other work done that needs to be done. So let's address this conundrum.

First, schedule effective conversations. If you really want to give a person your undivided attention, put it on your calendar and view it as a scheduled, "formal" task.

Second, leave open times in your schedule so that you can allow your colleagues or employees a chance to speak to you at some length about issues and problems that arise unexpectedly. Without some open times, you can end up with the habit of being efficient frequently with those around you. And that can push people away from you in a big way.

Third, when you conclude that you cannot spare the time to speak to another person in an effective conversation, be sure to explain it to the person:

> *"Mika, I'm sorry but I can't take the time right now to speak to you. I have to finish this incident report by 3 p.m. today and it's going to take quite a bit of time to do it."*

> *"Tania, I know you really want to talk to me now, and I appreciate that, but I am already late for a lunch meeting with a new prospect, and I've got to go. Let's talk when I get back."*

You may be saying the above words to Tania as you're walking toward the elevator. No matter. The important part is that you are showing respect for her by explaining that you realize you're being efficient and do not want her to take it personally.

Emails

Given that there are excellent websites today providing great tips for managing email well, we would like to present just two ideas for you to consider:

First, to be really efficient, consider using SLO, that is, write only a subject line, with no text at all in the body of the email. SLO means "Subject Line Only." What we're doing in effect is sending a text message in the email system.

> From: Joe Coyle and Joe Hospital
> To: Elliott Thomas
> Cc:
> Subject: SLO: We will finish our interviews tomorrow morning and call you before noon.

As far as we know, we are the only people using this approach—but we have not had even one complaint from our clients, colleagues, et al. Our guess is that they appreciate the efficiency of it.

Second, to be both efficient and effective, write a functional ending to your full emails whenever possible. For example:

> *"In closing, now that we have agreed on a price for the software support service, the next step is for us to write up an agreement, which we will send to you by this coming Friday."*

> *"So, we will sit tight until you email us the exact dates of the 10K race, after which we will begin immediately working with your staff in New York City on the logistics."*

> *"If you would like to make any changes to the agenda, please do so by May 24th. If we do not hear from you, we will begin sending out materials to the attendees on May 25th."*

The goal here is to end the email trail. Once the other person knows the next step or what is going to happen, etc., he or she does not have to respond with yet another email. Unfortunately, we have found that, in many instances, writing such functional email endings is not easy—and may explain why so many of us lean too heavily on the perfunctory ending, "If you have any questions, do not hesitate to call."

But making the effort to write a real functional ending is good business since it enables everyone to know what's next, what will or won't happen, and what they have to do or not do.

Your Turn

Write two "functional" endings that could end an email you recently sent out or could be sent out over the next few days. To help you, we'd like to offer three often-used introductory elements: "In closing..."; "Moving forward..."; and "As a next step..."

Open-Door Policy

Any leader who establishes an open-door policy should realize that he or she is choosing effectiveness over efficiency. And it may be a good idea to do so. But this approach invites regular interruptions and can make it difficult for a leader to complete his or her routine work. The result can be long work days and weeks:

> *"Many days, I have to stay very late at work because I simply can't get any focused, quality work done with all the interruptions I get during the day. As the designated team leader, I am expected to help everyone with tough issues right away. As a*

result, I often have to go to my office on Saturday mornings when there's nobody around—and I find they are the most productive four hours of my week."

When a leader with an open-door policy comes to us concerned about his or her productivity, we advise establishing a compromise: Set specific hours for allowing interruptions (e.g., 12:30 p.m. to 3:30 p.m.), realizing that most of us need time to focus on all the routine work that piles up. In short, we all need time to be efficient.

Rush Periods/Slow Periods

Some businesses are structurally organized around this framework. In a full-service restaurant, for example, during "rush" periods (e.g., 11:45 a.m. to 1:30 p.m.) managers need to be unusually efficient. They can't take the time to deal with employee problems or to give extensive training and coaching. Usually, there's not even time to chat for five minutes. But after the rush (e.g., 2 p.m. to 4 p.m.) the leader can make a shift to a more effective, engaging style—asking good questions, hearing people out, teaching new low-skill staff about the business, or thinking of ways to increase sales and profits. Many managers find it difficult to make this transition. Rather, they continue working with intense efficiency even when the business is slow, which reduces their ability to add value to their team members.

This pattern can be a daily feature not only in restaurants but in hospital emergency rooms, or it can be seasonal as in accounting firms, florist businesses, and tourist attractions—even in farming and ranching. What's important for leaders in such situations to realize is that "there is a time to be efficient and a time to be effective."

Choosing Effectiveness at the Highest Levels

Given the heavy schedules of the highest-level leaders, many miss out on a valuable way to add value to their business: walking around with high touch.

Employees at all levels appreciate an opportunity to interact with their upper-level leaders. However, many leaders spend so much time in strategic meetings, in airplanes and in dealing with impatient clients that it is not easy for them to find time to "high touch" their employees. However, despite leading major companies, some corporate executives excel in high-touch interactions and, in doing so, build companies with high morale and lower turnover.

Given how busy you probably are, it is important to have a strategy for carrying out these effective high-touch interactions. We can offer one that a number of successful leaders use to maximize the number of employees they "touch" each month and year. They attend the opening session of regional meetings or training events and take just 5 minutes to express their thanks to the groups and provide some insight into the company's performance or future: products or services in the pipeline, upcoming changes in the organization, insights into the marketplace and the like. In this way, they reach a large number of employees without investing a great deal of time to do it.

Your Turn

Thinking about your past week or two of work, identify those times or instances when you chose *efficiency* and those when you chose *effectiveness.*

I chose efficiency:

1. ____________________

2. ____________________

3. ____________________

4. ____________________

5. ____________________

I chose effectiveness:

1. ______

2. ______

3. ______

4. ______

5. ______

Routine Work and Added-Value Activities

As you may have already guessed, this *efficiency* vs. *effectiveness* framework can be applied to the framework that opens this book:

ROUTINE WORK (Focus on *efficiency*)	→	"FIRES"	→	ADDING VALUE (Focus on *effectiveness*)

In general, we should aim to be efficient when completing our routine work (and when dealing with our "fires") and effective when completing our added-value activities or roles. Put simply, we should get through our routine emails so that we can spend as much time as possible driving results through creative thinking, creative problem solving, organizational development, people development, strategic planning, trend analysis, client engagement, and so on.

As we've mentioned earlier, although this framework may appear commonsensical and, therefore, easy to apply, leaders tell us it is not:

> *"Once I get rolling with my emails, paperwork and other 'gut' work, I get in a mode that makes me somewhat abrupt with my team. I have trouble relaxing or calming down because there is so much to do. I'm either worried about preparing for the next conference call or about finding the time to attend it. My team must find me to be a whirlwind, and I'm afraid my overly efficient work style wears them out a bit sometimes."*

> *"It seems that every year in our business there are more reports, more updates and more meetings. My days are packed. It seems that the only time I get to think deeply about how to improve myself and my team is when I'm driving home in the evenings. But I should be setting aside time during the day to think and plan like a leader. Somehow, the environment doesn't allow it to happen."*

These two executives are caught in a work life of intense efficiency. It's as if their productivity score, after each 11- or 12-hour day, remains a 70. Not bad—but not leadership level either.

Remedy

Leaders who succeed in finding time to be effective and, as a result, end up with two or three days a week with productivity scores above 90, report that they have to consciously choose one or two value-added activities from the digital list they put on their laptop or smart phone. On average, they report finding at least one or two hours each day to invest in those activities. Finding that time is not easy for them, but whenever successful, the effective, added-value work makes their day substantially more rewarding.

Epilogue

Final Thoughts

Final Thoughts

As a leader in our very challenging digital/information age, you will agree, we believe, that the success of any business or organization ultimately depends on the decision-making, problem solving, and creative thinking that leaders like you carry out. We refer to these activities as added value.

As we have pointed out a number of times, the modern workplace generates so much routine work and creates so many unplanned "fires" that many leaders cannot play the role they have been assigned to play. Accordingly, we have presented six frameworks by which you can systematically evaluate your role, workload, work conditions and output, as well as your people, so that you can develop better strategies for adding value in your leadership role.

Working with so many responsible managers and executives like you, we have found that these frameworks can help you identify ways to improve results and outcomes for your organization. We hope, therefore, that you will find the time to revisit and review the frameworks as well as the input you added to the various chapters.

Notes